THE MAP TO LIFE

...from trauma to Happiness

by

Yogi Sally Ann Slight

ISBN 978-1910123-423

2020
© SAS Publishing
Dartmouth, Devon UK

With the greatest of respect and thanks to...
Dr David Hawkins and his Process.
St Francis of Assisi.
Raymond Holliwell.

My Mother and myself, for wanting to be Happy.

Thanks Dad

What you are looking for, is where you are looking from.

St Francis of Assisi

EMOTIONAL SPIRAL

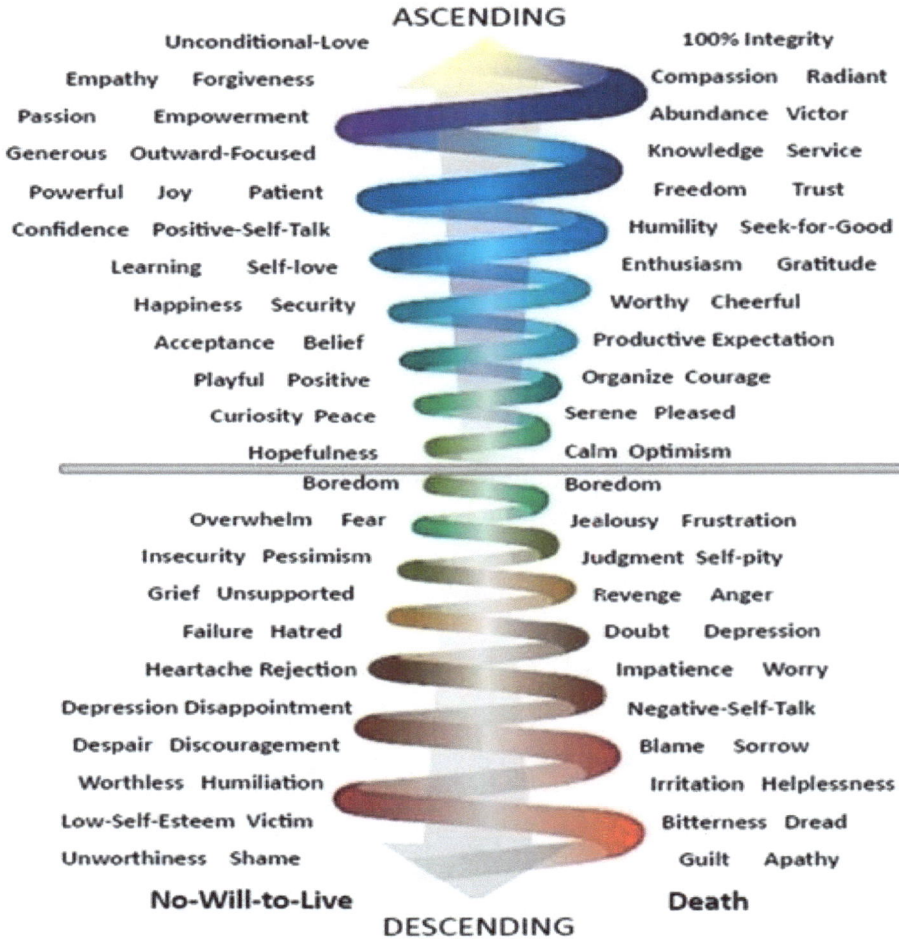

ASCENDING

Unconditional-Love	100% Integrity
Empathy Forgiveness	Compassion Radiant
Passion Empowerment	Abundance Victor
Generous Outward-Focused	Knowledge Service
Powerful Joy Patient	Freedom Trust
Confidence Positive-Self-Talk	Humility Seek-for-Good
Learning Self-love	Enthusiasm Gratitude
Happiness Security	Worthy Cheerful
Acceptance Belief	Productive Expectation
Playful Positive	Organize Courage
Curiosity Peace	Serene Pleased
Hopefulness	Calm Optimism
Boredom	Boredom
Overwhelm Fear	Jealousy Frustration
Insecurity Pessimism	Judgment Self-pity
Grief Unsupported	Revenge Anger
Failure Hatred	Doubt Depression
Heartache Rejection	Impatience Worry
Depression Disappointment	Negative-Self-Talk
Despair Discouragement	Blame Sorrow
Worthless Humiliation	Irritation Helplessness
Low-Self-Esteem Victim	Bitterness Dread
Unworthiness Shame	Guilt Apathy
No-Will-to-Live	**Death**

DESCENDING

**This Map is the inspiration for my
Good Health & Happiness,
and why I had to write this book
to help others.**

By remembering how sad I had been in the past,
I can see how long it took me to get to
the Happiness I feel now,
and the Process that I had to follow...even when I did
not even realize that I was
in a Process!

Yes, there is a Process that takes you
up into Happiness,
when you are feeling guilty, anxious or depressed.

Some are lucky enough to just,
'Know the Process'.

Others don't even know there is a Process!

...some refuse to be shown,
and so suffer through their life.

Many have now learnt to follow the Process,
and remain in the emotion they wish to remain in,
rather than keep flowing
from one emotion to another.

**Being born, and not given the Map to Life,
is just like being placed in Australia
and then told to go to England
...without a map!**

A Garden is the ultimate metaphor for your recovery.

The trauma garden is now full of weeds,
a whole mass of thought weeds from the incident,
and growing quicker the more you think about,
debate, write about and remember it.

**It is now time for you to choose,
Thought weeds or Thought flowers.**

And with the right focus,
your Good Life can be recovered again by
planting, tending and caring for your Good Life Garden,
to create a Garden/Life you will love living.

The sooner you start planting the flower Thoughts
in your Mind/garden again,
the sooner you start to feel better!

.

.

Everything that has happened to you,
had caused a shock wave within the body
...and that doesn't feel good does it?

And because you don't feel good,
you tend to keep saying "I don't feel good."

And then you have to state why you don't feel good,
because some people want to know the worst,
rather than return you to happiness quicker.

You can be sucked into the land of...
"Tell me all about it"
to aid them in some way,
rather than aid you!

This is all about you my dear,
so let's get you out of trauma quicker!

Shock comes from a quick life change.
You were happy and fun, then something comes along and
tips your world upside down.
.
.
So...
you can either sit and talk about it again and again,
(weeds) which creates more of the same feelings!
or...
you can sit and start to think about all the things you love.

You will still feel the body in shock,
as it takes time to turn that disturbance around.

And then, as you start to picture and speak about
all the things you love *(flowers)*,
you will start to turn your life back to good again...sooner.

...SMILE...
So, what do you love?

puppies... kittens... ice cream... flowers ...cars
anything you love?

...SMILE...
Sit and speak about all the things you love.
Picture them in your mind.
Get pictures of them from books and stare at them.
Write about kittens and puppies, cars etc.

...SMILE...
And then you start to feel deep down inside of you
that Good Love feeling you feel,
when you think, speak and write about
kittens, puppies and ice cream etc.

.

.

After trauma,
the remains of the Good Life garden
get more decayed the longer you focus
in the weed trauma garden.

**To weed a trauma garden you neglect it, totally,
and only feed the Good Life garden.**

And in this time of crisis,
we don't bother with seeds to grow new flowers,
we buy in whole pot plants!!
shrubs and full grown trees to rebuild it sooner,
to its former glory.
In our mind,
we get kittens and puppies to run around it,
build swings and tree houses to play in,
we buy a hot tub and anything we want to refurnish our
Good Life garden again.

**To focus on the good,
reduces the bad.
As you can only think one thought at a time.**

It is always your choice to think a better feeling thought.
OK, your body and Mind is trying to work out
why all that trauma happened to you,
to tell everyone about how horrid it was,
who is to blame and they should be punished etc.

And so...
you remain in the bad weeds and plant more of them,
which then creates dis-ease and sickness
and that makes you feel worse,
because you stayed in the weeds
...because you don't know how to remove the weeds,
you just keep growing more of them!

You don't even know you have a choice, do you?

The roots of weeds can only be removed
by complete lack of attention to them.
Do not water them in Thought or Word.

When a weed pops back into your mind,
as they will do,
you instantly think of a kitten or puppy,
car, or whatever you love!

Only you can do this for yourself.
It is always your choice to change your mind.

And as you start to think about kittens etc.
you have no thought of the past incident.

You may still feel that past thought;
as a bad thought sends a shock through you again,
so you feel bad again,
and start thinking bad thoughts again.
So...
that lower thought shock feeling is only overcome
by kitten and puppy power!
...SMILE...
Love is a higher vibrational level than trauma!

Your body shock is of low vibrational value,
and so to counteract that effect you have to oppose it,
with the higher vibrational love thoughts
which turn to feelings as you understand.

...because even understanding is a higher vibration
than your shock.
Just to be told the steps of how to move out of shock,
will bring you relief.

...SMILE...
*just as you train your muscles to grow and look good,
your SMILE trains your thoughts to create good emotions.*

Are you are still in a weed Thought trauma?

You CHOOSE to flow into the Good Life Garden

by changing your thoughts to good thoughts,
by speaking kind Words about the things you Love,
and forcing a **SMILE** onto your face.

The smile triggers all the good fluids
in the brain and body
and keeps the flow of love and kindness
flowing through you,
and into that Good Flower Garden you are recovering.

...trauma weeds will cling to you,
but only if you let them.

It is the Good work you have to do for yourself
to remain in a SMILE,
to think a good thought,
and do a kindness for another.
To overcome the lower memories
with higher feeling thoughts and words.

.

.

...SMILE...

The past has gone,
and every moment it goes further away,
when you chose to grow in the Good Thought Garden

...now, lets plant some veg!!
(another metaphor that you will understand later)

.

.

Here you sit, reading this book,
and so here you are in this moment NOW..................................reading.

You are safe,
You are warm *(perhaps)*,
You have everything you need in this moment NOW.
You may need a cup of tea *(you may already have one)*,
and
You are still in this moment NOW...reading.

Well done.

Because you have CHOSEN to sit and read this book NOW,
to focus upon these words you read NOW,

...you are in the moment of NOW!

All the words that I am writing to you are safe, kind and peaceful.

How are we going to explain something without a Word,
that creates more of what it is, because that is what Words do!

Let us know the truth about the word Trauma shall we?

Look at the word..Trauma

Let me explain the Word to you,
....the part of the word that creates, and you 'feel' when you read or say it
is...

'AUM'

In Yoga, **Aum** is the creation of Peace within you.
*THE PEACE IS ALWAYS WITHIN YOU...YOU ARE LOOKING OUTSIDE
OF YOURSELF FOR IT, YOUR THOUGHTS CREATED AN
EXPERIENCE, AND NOW YOU LOOK FOR PEACE OUTSIDE OF
SOMETHING THAT CREATES ALL THE PEACE YOU
NEED...YOU!*

.

And as you see in the word, tr**AUM**a, it sits within the Word that you use to explain an event from the past, that you have experienced, and seem to want to experience again....as you keep talking about it again!

And we have to understand why this is not a good idea.

AUM is the use of understanding the 'Word',
and the use of vibrations that occur within your body
and then into your outer life experience from using Words.

We use Words every moment of every day,
in thoughts that create feelings and emotions,
that create the words you use,
to communicate with others about how you feel,
or
all that you wish to explain to others.

There are good Words
and
there are bad Words.

Good because they make you FEEL good.
Bad because they make you FEEL bad...*it is not a bad Word, just a feeling.*

Your FEELINGS (vibrations) are just as important as Words, as they are what create the experiences that create your day to day life.

So,
**when you equate the word 'trauma' with bad experiences
you recreate those feelings again.
Those feelings recreate all the vibrations that you felt when you were
in that experience and made your life not pleasant.**

Those vibrations removed your innocence of Life.
It created a Life path that you have been travelling and that has now brought you to wanting to recreate your innocence again.

.

You are in the moment of Power where you can return to Innocence, Happiness and Love...
or
You can carry on, and get worse, deeper into the lower levels of emotion that create a life that you wish to leave now.

This very moment is the one where you decide...

Do you dig deeper into what happened in the past and so recreate all those vibrations that actually harm yourself,
or
You step kindly into the new Life you can create for yourself right NOW.

CONGRATULATIONS!

Ask yourself now...

Why do I really feel the need to share my hurt with another?

Does that other person deserve to feel the pain I have created in my mind?

When am I going to realize that the bad of the past has gone?

When am I going to tell myself a better story about the past?

When am I going to feel better?

.

.

When?

.

.

.

Now is a good time!

.

.

.

When you sit with another and talk you vibrate with them...what we mean is, every level of emotion has a vibrational rate that you emit just by thinking the thoughts that you think.
So, by feeling **'shame'** you are emitting a vibrational rate of approx 20 hz and that doesn't feel good does it.

By being in your company, you make them feel uncomfortable, if they are feeling happier than you.

And so they would rather bring you up to their level and help you to feel happy again...sooner!

How can they do that?

Well, listen to them...they know alot about being happy because they are;
You want to feel happy, so you have to learn how to be happy again.

'Yes but...', we hear you say, *'what about getting rid of my past?'*

Well, its a bit like learning Physics or Algebra, you don't sit talking about 2+2=4 for the whole day do you?
You listen, and learn step by step, how Physics is formulated;
you learn how to overcome 2+2 by thinking 8+8!

'Yes, but what about 2+2?' ...you keep on saying!

And so we say, 'Did you learn anything at school'?

'Yes, but the Doctor sent me to a place where we are to talk about the past trauma.'

And so why hasn't that worked for you?

Why are you here now reading this book wanting to be happy and understand why you do not talk about the past hurt you have suffered?

.

Because, just the same as all NEW knowledge has taken its time to be accepted by the masses, until it is **Accepted**, you are subjected to what they know and ask of you.
You trust them to know best for you, because you asked.

Things are changing all the time, and things will change for the better for you too.

There are some people that **Accept** and **Believe** that talking therapy is helpful to them.
Something shifts inside, and they get back on with life again.

Others, perhaps this includes you, are at another level and need to learn more because they want to know the Truth, and when you know the Truth, life gets better for you.

You say the past is the Truth ...because it happened to you.

Yes, but the Truth is... the past has gone *(the bad has gone).*

And yet you are not letting it go, because you need something else that the horridness gives you...

Attention.

When you cease to be, 'I want to be heard', or hope that something happens to someone or something in the past, as revenge, or that 'they must pay for all that they did', then you will know the Truth.

The Truth is... the bad in the past has gone.

There were thoughts and fears that enabled a series of events to take place in your past; you were either the Cause, or an Effect of the experience.

There is no need to explain all the events and how it led up to it, you sort that out in your everyday life, as you have moments of clarity that bring you the answers, and when you say that you do not want to have to experience them, then you do **need** to learn how to be happy; so that you can choose a better feeling thought the moment you are shown a moment of past that you needed an answer to.

So, sometimes, most times, it is best to say the bad of the past has gone. Because you will be given all the answers you require; you may not get them at the time you ask, because you are unable to handle the Truth at that time, so it is drip fed to you at times when you are in alignment with the Truth.

Only you know when that is, because you feel it, and it can either lift you in the Truth, or break you even more because you do not want to believe it.

So, it is best to start to **Accept** that the bad of the past has gone, and that you send only kindness and goodness in thoughts behind you, and look forward to a good future.

.

.

Now, here is a lesson in Happiness Physics,
and you will understand it only by repeating it to yourself,
as you did with 2+2 = 4.

Every Thought is a vibration...8
Every Word is a vibration..8

If we live by accepting every word of others on the TV, radio, newspapers and by mouth then we are accepting their vibrations of opinion and beliefs.

Just as you can accept the words I write, or not.
Just because everyone else does it, you do not have to.
It is a choice.
If you did not know that before, you do now!

Your own Thoughts and Words are also yours to **choose** and **Accept**,
and you mainly do so because they have gotten you this far
...but at what cost?

What emotional turmoil have you experienced from Thought and Word?
And I really don't want you to explain, as you are trying to lift yourself out of that torment and trauma now aren't you?

You are now at the new level of learning that will aid you in your journey to Happiness, Peace or even Love!
Oh yes, you can feel everything again ...and you get to choose.

You just need a Map.

In life you need a map if you are going somewhere you have not been before, or maybe to get you back to somewhere you loved, because you feel you are lost.

In Mathematics you need a formula to help you achieve an understanding of the Process.
Everything is about learning a formula or following a guide, from someone who has achieved the goal or destination before, and has made life easier for you...and then life flows easier for you!

Some want to learn the old way, on their own terms and find a better route.
Why?
It has already been done for you!

You can have such a good life when your thoughts are Good and you feel better. It will just take you some time to understand a new way of thinking, and that is also your choice.

So we have written this Map/Guide/Process/Formula...

...to make life easier for you.

You can adjust it to your own understanding, but as we have learnt by Comparison in life already, **Peace** feels a whole lot better than **shame**, and when you have a Map, life just gets that bit easier than it was before you Accepted any help.

.

I have found **'being Thankful'** lifts you higher, and **'Smiling'** also aids you in reaching a higher level, than the one you are on now.

You can find other emotions and place them where you know they fit above or below, and keep track of your progress in reaching your goal.

Sometimes some people don't want to be happy, and have found they get more attention being cared for in grief, so they prolong their stay there, not realizing that it can have adverse affects on future Good Health, Happiness and Pleasure in life, if they remain in a low emotion for too long.

As we have said before, it is always a choice, and you will always find you are attracted to people that 'vibe' at the same level as you, or you may feel discomfort to someone on a different level.

You perhaps knew this before, you just didn't understand why, or even created a story about the person, so you could be proven right about them, when really all they needed was some direction to Happiness just like you.

Well, now they have, and so do you !
...and you will feel happier by being more Compassionate to someone who feels lower than you, and you can also guide them as you have been, so that they too can 'pay it forward' and help others to Happiness and Love too.

Bon Voyage!
.

.

.

.

.

EMOTIONAL SPIRAL

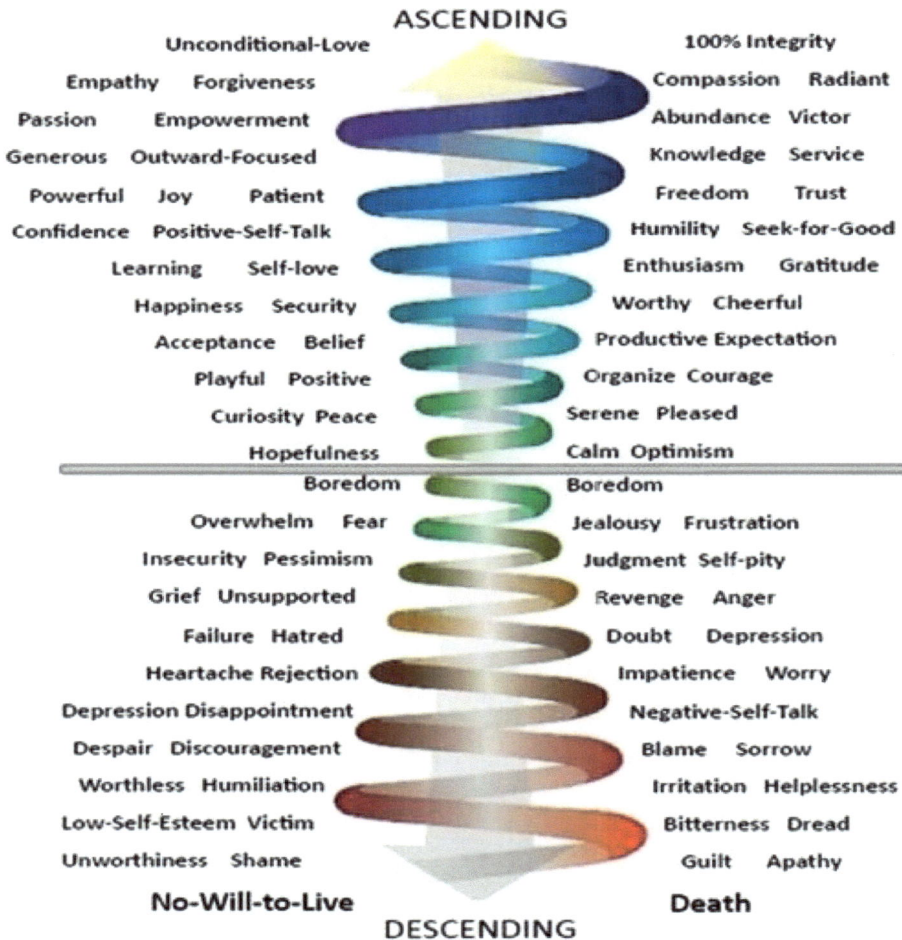

ASCENDING

Unconditional-Love

Empathy   Forgiveness

Passion   Empowerment

Generous   Outward-Focused

Powerful   Joy   Patient

Confidence   Positive-Self-Talk

Learning   Self-love

Happiness   Security

Acceptance   Belief

Playful   Positive

Curiosity   Peace

Hopefulness

100% Integrity

Compassion   Radiant

Abundance   Victor

Knowledge   Service

Freedom   Trust

Humility   Seek-for-Good

Enthusiasm   Gratitude

Worthy   Cheerful

Productive   Expectation

Organize   Courage

Serene   Pleased

Calm   Optimism

Boredom

Overwhelm   Fear

Insecurity   Pessimism

Grief   Unsupported

Failure   Hatred

Heartache   Rejection

Depression   Disappointment

Despair   Discouragement

Worthless   Humiliation

Low-Self-Esteem   Victim

Unworthiness   Shame

Boredom

Jealousy   Frustration

Judgment   Self-pity

Revenge   Anger

Doubt   Depression

Impatience   Worry

Negative-Self-Talk

Blame   Sorrow

Irritation   Helplessness

Bitterness   Dread

Guilt   Apathy

No-Will-to-Live   **Death**

DESCENDING

The Map of Ascension

Vibrational (Hz) levels of Emotion and how to get there...

Goal	Hz	Process
Unconditional Love	1000	100% Integrity
Peace	900	Compassion
Passion	800	Abundance
Bliss	750	Illumination
Joy	700	Trust
Love	650	Freedom
Learning	600	Gratitude
Happiness & Belief	550	Worthiness
Forgiveness & Positivity	500	Acceptance
Serenity	400	Pleasure
Hopefulness	300	Calm & Intention
boredom	***200***	Release
pride & scorn	175	inflation
hate & anger	150	aggression
craving & disappointment	125	enslavement
anxiety & fear	100	withdrawal
grief & regret	75	despondency
apathy & despair	50	helplessness
guilt & blame	30	destruction
shame & humiliation	20	elimination
sickness	10	Thankfulness
death	---	**Want to Live**

.

.

.

.

Now, let's start with...

'death'

...at the very bottom of the list, and the Process of how you can rise up out of it, shall we!

.

death = termination or destruction; a state of affairs; as if afraid of one's life.

When you feel like **death**....*(hopefully you have never got this low, but if you have reached this level, and survived!),* you know how bad everything really can be, and you must assure yourself that there can be nothing that feels any worse than death.
And so just by knowing this, and having the lowest Comparison of all, it can help you feel a bit better when you are in **shame** and **humiliation** or **sickness**, because you know you are on a higher level than feeling like death...so that is a good thing!

So, now you must understand that there is always something lower than what you feel now, and just by knowing that can make you feel better about yourself again...*(unless you are really dead, and then you are!).* This happens through Comparison, and so you can even get a little **Joy** from knowing you had to go through that level so you could understand how it feels, and so you can decide to not go there again!

Remember, it is always your choice of emotional level that you wish to experience, it really is what you choose to feel like today, and that wanting is the momentum required to raise you up out of the 'literal pit' or even drop you back in it again.

When you find yourself down there emotionally, it only needs YOU to remember and say...
"I CHOOSE TO FEEL BETTER, HAPPY, KIND, LOVING etc."
"I am healthy, loving, kind, good, peaceful etc."
Smile, and then you are on your way.

And keeping a higher level is only through practice and *WILL POWER.* The power of your will to live is greater than death, it overcomes all lower thought...*(your body on the other hand is liable to death, and if you have broken it beyond repair, then you have learnt a lesson...**think good thoughts to keep a Good body).***

So, you are on the next level out of death *(as your body is still capable of life)*.........Phew, that feels better, and yet you have now found yourself in...
.

The Map of Ascension

Vibrational (Hz) levels of Emotion and how to get there...

Goal	Hz	Process
Unconditional Love	1000	100% Integrity
Peace	900	Compassion
Passion	800	Abundance
Bliss	750	Illumination
Joy	700	Trust
Love	650	Freedom
Learning	600	Gratitude
Happiness & Belief	550	Worthiness
Forgiveness & Positivity	500	Acceptance
Serenity	400	Pleasure
Hopefulness	300	Calm & Intention
boredom	***200***	Release
pride & scorn	175	inflation
hate & anger	150	aggression
craving & disappointment	125	enslavement
anxiety & fear	100	withdrawal
grief & regret	75	despondency
apathy & despair	50	helplessness
guilt & blame	30	destruction
shame & humiliation	20	elimination
sickness	**10**	**Thankfulness**
death	---	Want to Live

'**sickness**', which in itself feels better than death but not much, so the process can only be *THANKFULNESS* to get you out of sickness.

You have felt better in the past, *(oh yes you have!)*, remember when you felt in Good Health and Happiness, and seeing as you have nothing else to do whilst you are sick than to think, you may as well think good thoughts; and memories have a great part to play in raising you up out of your sickness, because the other way is death isn't it!

.

Once again, this is all your choice!

SMILE & BE THANKFUL, not in an urgent and anxious pleading of thanks, but by truly being thankful for Good Health, Good Times and Happiness.

And in the **calm** of the moment you raise your vibrational levels up into the higher levels of Good Health, even to Peace, and that always feels good and is a short cut to the higher levels of emotion....wooo hooo!

Remember, being sick is a very low vibration and opens you up to other sickness and contagion, so get out as soon as you can...

Smile.

Many sickness' are created by the lower thoughts and emotions, and so by you staying in the higher levels of emotion will keep you in Good Health thankfully.

(I have written other books about sickness, so you can use them for more information about understanding your higher emotions and how to get there).

.

.

.

'THANKFULNESS' is being grateful and appreciative; responsible for ones words *(so make them good ones)*.

What are you really thankful for at this moment ?

.

The Map of Ascension

Vibrational (Hz) levels of Emotion and how to get there...

Goal	Hz	Process
Unconditional Love	1000	100% Integrity
Peace	900	Compassion
Passion	800	Abundance
Bliss	750	Illumination
Joy	700	Trust
Love	650	Freedom
Learning	600	Gratitude
Happiness & Belief	550	Worthiness
Forgiveness & Positivity	500	Acceptance
Serenity	400	Pleasure
Hopefulness	300	Calm & Intention
boredom	***200***	Release
pride & scorn	175	inflation
hate & anger	150	aggression
craving & disappointment	125	enslavement
anxiety & fear	100	withdrawal
grief & regret	75	despondency
apathy & despair	50	helplessness
guilt & blame	30	destruction
shame & humiliation	**20**	**elimination**
sickness	10	Thankfulness
death	---	Want to Live

'shame and humiliation' come from your despising and being miserable about yourself, life situations and experiences.
Feeling unworthy with low self-esteem.

Why?

.

You are lovely and perhaps things have happened to you that you wish had not *(and this is where we came in at the beginning of the book),* but they have happened and they are now past and you are not dead, you may be sick but you now know how to overcome that too, so we have to *ELIMINATE* this level for you to rise up out of it.

You have done nothing wrong. Really, even if you think you have, you have not. It is past, it is gone it is *ELIMINATED* by another level.
You can stay at this level as long as you want, working out the whys and who did what to who, but does it feel good?

And so to eliminate this fully we must step up into the next level...

ELIMINATION is to remove or take out; to reject or omit from consideration *(just as you can choose to not believe what you read here);* to expel.
Not just physically, mentally remove thoughts that create your experience.

As soon as you possibly can...like NOW!

...and you can only **ELIMINATE** a thought by choosing another to take its place....so make it a good one.

SMILE...they come easier that way.

(and if you think really good thoughts, you can skip the next step too...)!

.

The Map of Ascension

Vibrational (Hz) levels of Emotion and how to get there...

Goal	Hz	Process
Unconditional Love	1000	100% Integrity
Peace	900	Compassion
Passion	800	Abundance
Bliss	750	Illumination
Joy	700	Trust
Love	650	Freedom
Learning	600	Gratitude
Happiness & Belief	550	Worthiness
Forgiveness & Positivity	500	Acceptance
Serenity	400	Pleasure
Hopefulness	300	Calm & Intention
boredom	***200***	Release
pride & scorn	175	inflation
hate & anger	150	aggression
craving & disappointment	125	enslavement
anxiety & fear	100	withdrawal
grief & regret	75	despondency
apathy & despair	50	helplessness
guilt & blame	**30**	**destruction**
shame & humiliation	20	elimination
sickness	10	Thankfulness
death	---	Want to Live

'guilt and blame' which comes from being vindictive and evil in thought, word and deed, it is *DESTRUCTIVE* to your health and can lose you your friends and family, it really is not a level to hang around on for long but it does feel better than misery and shame...

or

you can *FORGIVE !*

.

By **DE*STRUCTION*****!** to destroy for safety; the act of destroying a cause; intending without positive suggestions of help;

Yes, you are de**struct**ing your internal body by being negative and remaining in the lower levels of thought emotion.
And yet you can **destroy** your lower thoughts to rise you up and out of these lower levels; therefore recon**struct**ing your internal organs by your better feeling thoughts, that come when you rise up into higher levels of thoughts and emotions...of your own choosing.

So, **DE*STRUCTION*** is Good, and bad in terms of Thought.
How fantastic is that!

A really useful Word that when used correctly, can recon**struct** by the correct in**struct**ions.

You can self-de**struct**
You can recon**struct**

It is always your choice of direction in using this Map of In**struct**ion.

The process of ***FORGIVENESS*** rises you up over all the lower emotions and into Positivity which always feels fantastic, and is kindness to yourself and to others.

*(**FORGIVENESS** really means that you have let the past go...it is GONE! and it feels wonderfully freeing and peaceful....try it!)*

And if you still haven't **Forgiven** we are now in...

.

The Map of Ascension

Vibrational (Hz) levels of Emotion and how to get there...

Goal	Hz	Process
Unconditional Love	1000	100% Integrity
Peace	900	Compassion
Passion	800	Abundance
Bliss	750	Illumination
Joy	700	Trust
Love	650	Freedom
Learning	600	Gratitude
Happiness & Belief	550	Worthiness
Forgiveness & Positivity	500	Acceptance
Serenity	400	Pleasure
Hopefulness	300	Calm & Intention
boredom	***200***	Release
pride & scorn	175	inflation
hate & anger	150	aggression
craving & disappointment	125	enslavement
anxiety & fear	100	withdrawal
grief & regret	75	despondency
apathy & despair	**50**	**helplessness**
guilt & blame	30	destruction
shame & humiliation	20	elimination
sickness	10	Thankfulness
death	---	Want to Live

'apathy and despair' that comes from not Forgiving, feeling hopeless that you don't know how to move from this level and condemning yourself and all the others involved.

The process to go higher and out of apathy and despair is ***ABDICATION***

.

ABDICATE is to renounce responsibility, rights etc. especially formally.

...Yes, just like King Edward VIII abdicated the throne of England so he could, 'be with the women he loved.' (*but can you be bothered?)*...

Is it so difficult to find 'something' or someone to focus upon and to love them?

To *LOVE* is also a process, that lifts you up out of the lower levels of emotion up into the emotion of Love...so to use an emotion as a process is also a very great way to understand and rise up out of these lower levels.

Maybe you can't *LOVE* your past *(yet!)* or *FORGIVE*...

The Process of **HELPLESSNESS** means you are unable to manage independently; you have been made weak by past thoughts and **Helplessness** is abdicating your rights to using your own will power and thoughts, by taking advice from another and to be helped by them.

Only you know if you are thinking your own thoughts, or you are using the advice/thoughts of another in this situation.

SMILE...breathe deeply and slowly, and be thankful you are safe now. Where you are right now is correct, and as you remain in this calm you will know the next correct thought to take....as it feels good.

You can *ABDICATE* your seat of thoughts of Helplessness on this level, to the higher level of...

.

The Map of Ascension

Vibrational (Hz) levels of Emotion and how to get there...

Goal	Hz	Process
Unconditional Love	1000	100% Integrity
Peace	900	Compassion
Passion	800	Abundance
Bliss	750	Illumination
Joy	700	Trust
Love	650	Freedom
Learning	600	Gratitude
Happiness & Belief	550	Worthiness
Forgiveness & Positivity	500	Acceptance
Serenity	400	Pleasure
Hopefulness	300	Calm & Intention
boredom	***200***	Release
pride & scorn	175	inflation
hate & anger	150	aggression
craving & disappointment	125	enslavement
anxiety & fear	100	withdrawal
grief & regret	**75**	**despondency**
apathy & despair	50	helplessness
guilt & blame	30	destruction
shame & humiliation	20	elimination
sickness	10	Thankfulness
death	---	Want to Live

'grief and regret' which comes from not Forgiving, Loving and believing in your tragedy more than your Good Health and Happiness

(...and your regret is a kinder feeling than despair isn't it? ....phew!)

.

Perhaps you regret how you were where you were, when it happened, but once again it is the past, and we have *ELIMINATED* that level, we have *DESTROYED* it, we have *ABDICATED* ourselves from those lower levels and even if we haven't Forgiven them (yet) we are now higher than shame, guilt, blame, humiliation and despair and even if our spirits are low from lack of courage in *DESPONDENCY,* it is just by acknowledging that, and that will give us the momentum once again to get up and out, and into......

DESPONDENCY is being downcast or disheartened; dejected; in despair. and is a better feeling than Helplessness!

...so that is something to be thankful about, and you have risen up into grief and regret from your apathy and helplessness....Yay!

And yet, it still doesn't feel too good does it?

Shall we move on quickly out of this level?
...or do you still want to talk about the past trauma and stay longer?

...and the longer you stay, the worse you feel, and you may start to sink lower again...and yet it is always your choice, to stay here and talk about all the hurt you suffered, or to forgive the past and step on upwards and feel better sooner...it is always your choice.
.
.
.
.
.
.
.

...are you ready?

.

The Map of Ascension

Vibrational (Hz) levels of Emotion and how to get there...

Goal	Hz	Process
Unconditional Love	1000	100% Integrity
Peace	900	Compassion
Passion	800	Abundance
Bliss	750	Illumination
Joy	700	Trust
Love	650	Freedom
Learning	600	Gratitude
Happiness & Belief	550	Worthiness
Forgiveness & Positivity	500	Acceptance
Serenity	400	Pleasure
Hopefulness	300	Calm & Intention
boredom	***200***	Release
pride & scorn	175	inflation
hate & anger	150	aggression
craving & disappointment	125	enslavement
anxiety & fear	**100**	**withdrawal**
grief & regret	75	despondency
apathy & despair	50	helplessness
guilt & blame	30	destruction
shame & humiliation	20	elimination
sickness	10	Thankfulness
death	---	Want to Live

'anxiety and fear' *(really, did you ever think you would look forward to fear and anxiety, rather than stay in shame, despair or grief??*

Amazing isn't it!
Come on, you must be smiling at that last remark?....Please!).

.

So, now we are in the level of 'fear' and we are 'anxious' about what?
What can be so frightening about now?

Why do we feel the need to punish ourselves further by our own thoughts,
or are we fearful about the thoughts/advice from another?
...as there is no one doing anything harmful to us in this moment now is
there?

Remember, a thought is just a thought,
from past memories *(good or bad),*
a judgement about this moment now,
a dream or worry about the future...
and it is only when you accept it and believe it, that you experience its
power.

SMILE to experience good thoughts that feel better.

WITHDRAWAL is an act or Process of withdrawing; to take, draw back
or away; remove; retract; retreat; to depart; to detach oneself socially,
mentally or emotionally...so that you can have some space to sit with your
thoughts, your beliefs and ask each one...
'Do you feel good?'

...and then choose whether you keep that thought or not.
As a bad feeling thought can ruin your day,
just as a good feeling thought can make a whole day better.

It is always your choice in which direction you choose to make your day.

We have the option to **Forgive** and **Love** ourselves again if we so choose.

Surely, after all that we have just been through to get us to this level, we
can *WITHDRAW* from being anxious and fearful,
because we know we can now rise up out of the 'fear' by choosing a better
feeling thought, and so rise up to the higher level and into....

.

The Map of Ascension

Vibrational (Hz) levels of Emotion and how to get there...

Goal	Hz	Process
Unconditional Love	1000	100% Integrity
Peace	900	Compassion
Passion	800	Abundance
Bliss	750	Illumination
Joy	700	Trust
Love	650	Freedom
Learning	600	Gratitude
Happiness & Belief	550	Worthiness
Forgiveness & Positivity	500	Acceptance
Serenity	400	Pleasure
Hopefulness	300	Calm & Intention
boredom	***200***	Release
pride & scorn	175	inflation
hate & anger	150	aggression
craving & disappointment	**125**	**enslavement**
anxiety & fear	100	withdrawal
grief & regret	75	despondency
apathy & despair	50	helplessness
guilt & blame	30	destruction
shame & humiliation	20	elimination
sickness	10	Thankfulness
death	---	Want to Live

'craving and disappointment' ....*Wow, what a great choice!*

as it is still a better feeling than, fear and being anxious, because
disappointment comes from denying our own craving and desires.

.

Even if you don't get what you **desire** and crave, at least you tried!
You have tried to gain a **desire** haven't you???.....*Really!?*

Imagine going through life without even making an attempt or reaching for
all you **desire**, or even one thing you **desire**.

Just by thinking about what you **desire** has *WITHDRAWN* you from
fearful thoughts and anxiety of not knowing an outcome.
...and that feels so much better doesn't it!

So, to try for something you **desire**, crave or just want a bit of something,
feels better than 'fear and anxiety', despair and apathy.

And just knowing that, is a relief for any anxious thought,
and *that really is worth remembering!*

Remember... do not be in *ENSLAVEMENT* to your desires.

ENSLAVEMENT is to make a slave of; to subjugate; be subservient;
submissive; use consideration, as it may be the decision/desire of another!

Do not deny yourself an opportunity to try for your desire, *as that also
feels bad;* an opportunity gives you the time to choose for yourself.
...and if you do become Enslaved to your desires, you may get stuck on
this level.

Smile...you will be ok.

You can **Forgive** yourself and **Love** a higher level of emotion, and then
choose to go up another level into...

.

The Map of Ascension

Vibrational (Hz) levels of Emotion and how to get there...

Goal	Hz	Process
Unconditional Love	1000	100% Integrity
Peace	900	Compassion
Passion	800	Abundance
Bliss	750	Illumination
Joy	700	Trust
Love	650	Freedom
Learning	600	Gratitude
Happiness & Belief	550	Worthiness
Forgiveness & Positivity	500	Acceptance
Serenity	400	Pleasure
Hopefulness	300	Calm & Intention
boredom	***200***	Release
pride & scorn	175	inflation
hate & anger	**150**	**aggression**
craving & disappointment	125	enslavement
anxiety & fear	100	withdrawal
grief & regret	75	despondency
apathy & despair	50	helplessness
guilt & blame	30	destruction
shame & humiliation	20	elimination
sickness	10	Thankfulness
death	---	Want to Live

'hate and anger' ...*are you sure that is a higher level than desire and craving?.*

....Really?!

Yes, surprisingly hate and anger can raise you up out of your desire and craving because to hate yourself for perhaps spending too much money on a desire that was needed elsewhere, and to be angry at yourself for wasting so much time in pointless pursuits of no gain because this *AGGRESSION* has more energy behind it, that can create the momentum you require to release you from the lower emotion and disappointment.

AGGRESSION is an attack or harmful action; an offensive activity or practice etc. and used as a destructive mental attitude; assertive; vigorous.

When used against others, AGRESSION is not acceptable behaviour, but it does have the same momentum and energy that is required to reach a higher level of emotion, that feels better than disappointment and depression that can be caused by a wrong choice of desire.

You are the Cause of the desire, so **Forgive** yourself if you have made the wrong choice, and are suffering the Effects of that choice.

Do not make a habit of anger as you can become *ENSLAVED* in *AGGRESSION* too....*really not worth the loss of energy, friends and family is it?*

As long as you can control your anger, keep a lid on the boiler as it were, and use it wisely, you can rocket off to another level with ease....but it does take practice, and perhaps you get better at apologising to your loved ones. *(Show them this book so they too can understand why you felt the need to let off steam, as you were not proficient in Forgiveness, Love or the next higher level yet).*

In this moment NOW you can change direction, and choose a better feeling thought to relieve any anger, yet feel the power that changing your mind can bring and head you ever upwards...

SMILE...

And the next level up is.....

.

The Map of Ascension

Vibrational (Hz) levels of Emotion and how to get there...

Goal	Hz	Process
Unconditional Love	1000	100% Integrity
Peace	900	Compassion
Passion	800	Abundance
Bliss	750	Illumination
Joy	700	Trust
Love	650	Freedom
Learning	600	Gratitude
Happiness & Belief	550	Worthiness
Forgiveness & Positivity	500	Acceptance
Serenity	400	Pleasure
Hopefulness	300	Calm & Intention
boredom	***200***	Release
pride & scorn	**175**	**inflation**
hate & anger	150	aggression
craving & disappointment	125	enslavement
anxiety & fear	100	withdrawal
grief & regret	75	despondency
apathy & despair	50	helplessness
guilt & blame	30	destruction
shame & humiliation	20	elimination
sickness	10	Thankfulness
death	---	Want to Live

'pride and scorn' ...*Yes, pride is a lower level emotion, as it is easily INFLATED and can ruin a life*

...although it always feels better than anger and despair....Yay!

.

The only thing to be proud of now is the higher level you have achieved so far, and your indifference to your anger and hate, and be proud you kept the lid on the boiling pot of hateful thoughts of misunderstanding, that you created from your time in the lower emotional levels.

Remember, you overcame your revenge and hate so you can feel pride in yourself for that.

And yet, contempt and scorn are nothing to be proud of, as they come from you being too demanding of self or others. Scorn is an open contempt for a person or thing; an object of derision; to reject by contempt.
They are higher emotional levels than the hate and anger and should still be overcome as soon as possible.

Accepting that others views are just as valuable as your own, and once again by Forgiveness that the past has gone, and Love of self; pride that you now want to feel even better.

INFLATION is an act or state; a progressive increase; an Effect from expansion; to swell; to rise in spirits; elation..

Well done for your understanding your *INFLATED LOVE OF SELF;* a JOY that increases your vibrational rate

and raises you up to the next level of...

.

The Map of Ascension

Vibrational (Hz) levels of Emotion and how to get there...

Goal	Hz	Process
Unconditional Love	1000	100% Integrity
Peace	900	Compassion
Passion	800	Abundance
Bliss	750	Illumination
Joy	700	Trust
Love	650	Freedom
Learning	600	Gratitude
Happiness & Belief	550	Worthiness
Forgiveness & Positivity	500	Acceptance
Serenity	400	Pleasure
Hopefulness	300	Calm & Intention
boredom	*****200*****	**Release**
pride & scorn	175	inflation
hate & anger	150	aggression
craving & disappointment	125	enslavement
anxiety & fear	100	withdrawal
grief & regret	75	despondency
apathy & despair	50	helplessness
guilt & blame	30	destruction
shame & humiliation	20	elimination
sickness	10	Thankfulness
death	---	Want to Live

'boredom'.........*(I went to bed, I couldn't be bothered to tell you anymore, I might stay on this level for sometime as I have worked very hard lately and I need a rest...I choose to rest, I choose to not be bothered....I choose to do nothing at all....you can wait can't you?)*

.

Apparently not!
You want to feel Happier sooner don't you, and who can blame you.
Well done, a very good choice!

And so boredom, is like the doldrums at sea, when there is no wind to fill
the sails that gives your vessel the energy it requires to head you in the
direction of your choice...
Oh yes! It is still your choice.
You can stay here in the doldrums of boredom and allow the body and
mind to rest *(which is always a good plan, for a while at least),* or you can
fit an engine of **Knowledge/Passion/Love** as your *RELEASE* to your
vessel.

RELEASE to free from captivity or imprisonment; to free someone from
obligation or duty; to free from grip, to let fall; to issue for sale or
circulation; to make known; to relinquish a right or claim in favour of
someone else; a control mechanism for starting or stopping a machine.

The energy that is held within a favourite hobby/book/pastime or sport has
upon you, can *RELEASE* the energy you require to furl and stow the sails,
until you feel the need for them and the economy they provide again...*(and
they are quieter too, another opportunity of Peace).*

Boredom is the middle ground, the balance point, the place of safety where
you can once again choose to remain here, or head off in another direction
to return once again to your Happiness and Love.

Yes, you have been there before, and perhaps you feel Happiness and Love
hurt you, when actually they never can, it is just your thoughts about what
happened, and your lack of understanding that they too have choices that
created your fear of Happiness and Love.
And so the *COURAGE* required of you is to *RELEASE* yourself from this
level and up to.......

Hopefulness or back down to..**pride and scorn**
(are you experiencing a decision or indecision.....again?).

Hold my hand......................let's head onwards and upwards shall we......?!
.

The Map of Ascension

Vibrational (Hz) levels of Emotion and how to get there...

Goal	Hz	Process
Unconditional Love	1000	100% Integrity
Peace	900	Compassion
Passion	800	Abundance
Bliss	750	Illumination
Joy	700	Trust
Love	650	Freedom
Learning	600	Gratitude
Happiness & Belief	550	Worthiness
Forgiveness & Positivity	500	Acceptance
Serenity	400	Pleasure
Hopefulness	**300**	**Calm & Intention**
boredom	***200***	Release
pride & scorn	175	inflation
hate & anger	150	aggression
craving & disappointment	125	enslavement
anxiety & fear	100	withdrawal
grief & regret	75	despondency
apathy & despair	50	helplessness
guilt & blame	30	destruction
shame & humiliation	20	elimination
sickness	10	Thankfulness
death	---	Want to Live

'Hopefulness'.....*(and you can tell there has been a shift for the better, as we are now in Capital Letter land)!*.........*woooooo hooooooo!*

.

Phew! ...Do you feel it?

There feels like a fresher air about ourselves now we are in **Hopefulness**; that has come from the *INSPIRATION* of reading this book, and others like it you may have found useful, and the *WILLINGNESS* to want to improve your Life journey.

To look back at the list and see how far you have already come; to use all of those experiences as **Comparison**, and to know there is still quite some way to go to feeling a whole lot better, yet this has given you a fresher energy and more speed to get you to your goal....

But be careful, speed will get you where you want to go quickly, but you might miss some wonderful experiences on the way to your goal; so lets take it easy and feel the *SATISFACTION* of this journey, heading now in the right direction, and the *TRUST* that can be felt by knowing you only want the best for yourself now.

CONGRATULATIONS...

INTENTION a purpose or a goal; the act of intending; design or purpose with respect to a proposal; performed by expressing intention, deliberate; something that is intended, aim; firmly fixed, determined, concentrated; directing one's mind or energy.....and a natural healing process in which the edges of a wound cling together with no tissue between *(1st)* or the edges adhere with tissue between *(2nd)... Isn't knowledge fantastic!*

We are now in a state of *CALM (a different calm than the doldrums of boredom)* as our *INTENTION* is to press on

and up into the next level of......

.

The Map of Ascension

Vibrational (Hz) levels of Emotion and how to get there...

Goal	Hz	Process
Unconditional Love	1000	100% Integrity
Peace	900	Compassion
Passion	800	Abundance
Bliss	750	Illumination
Joy	700	Trust
Love	650	Freedom
Learning	600	Gratitude
Happiness & Belief	550	Worthiness
Forgiveness & Positivity	500	Acceptance
Serenity	**400**	**Pleasure**
Hopefulness	300	Calm & Intention
boredom	***200***	Release
pride & scorn	175	inflation
hate & anger	150	aggression
craving & disappointment	125	enslavement
anxiety & fear	100	withdrawal
grief & regret	75	despondency
apathy & despair	50	helplessness
guilt & blame	30	destruction
shame & humiliation	20	elimination
sickness	10	Thankfulness
death	---	Want to Live

'Serenity' *a level of PEACEFUL or TRANQUIL CALM, CLARITY and BRIGHTNESS*

A level where you now have knowledge of your choice of energy and where you can use this knowledge to remain *CALM* and travel onwards in Life with *OPTIMISM* and take *PLEASURE* in feeling good in this new found Super Power you have acquired; by just wanting to reach for the Happiness and Love that are already yours, waiting for you to get there.

Isn't this exciting?!!!...calmly excited!

Although *calmly excited* allows you to keep heading in the correct direction, and still experience all the *PLEASURES* along the way to your goal.

PLEASURE an agreeable or enjoyable sensation or emotion; something that gives enjoyment; amusement; recreation; a *personal* preference.

OPTIMISM is the tendency to expect the best in all things; hopefulness; confidence; the doctrine of the ultimate triumph of Good over evil; the philosophical doctrine that this is the best of all possible worlds.

REMAIN *CALM* and when you are ready you can enjoy *OPTIMUM PLEASURE* in the next level of...

.
.
.
.
.
.
.
.
.
.
.
.
.
.
.

...understandably you are not ready to leave yet are you!?

.

The Map of Ascension

Vibrational (Hz) levels of Emotion and how to get there...

Goal	Hz	Process
Unconditional Love	1000	100% Integrity
Peace	900	Compassion
Passion	800	Abundance
Bliss	750	Illumination
Joy	700	Trust
Love	650	Freedom
Learning	600	Gratitude
Happiness & Belief	550	Worthiness
Forgiveness & Positivity	**500**	**Acceptance**
Serenity	400	Pleasure
Hopefulness	300	Calm & Intention
boredom	***200***	Release
pride & scorn	175	inflation
hate & anger	150	aggression
craving & disappointment	125	enslavement
anxiety & fear	100	withdrawal
grief & regret	75	despondency
apathy & despair	50	helplessness
guilt & blame	30	destruction
shame & humiliation	20	elimination
sickness	10	Thankfulness
death	---	Want to Live

'**Forgiveness and Positivity**' expressing certainty or affirmation; real; possessing actual specific qualities; real; constructive; laudable; progress; improvement; in *Mathematics* having a value greater than zero; measured in a direction opposite to that regarded as negative; having the same magnitude as but opposite to an equivalent negative quality; in *Physics* as an electrical charge, having an opposite polarity to the charge of an electron and the same polarity as the charge of a proton; the results of a test indicating the presence of a suspected disorder or organism; in a *Photographic* image whose colours or tones correspond to those of the original subject.

We are finally here...**TRANSCENDENCE** is exceeding or surpassing in degree or excellence; beyond or before experience (Kant); having existence outside the created world; free from the limitations inherent in matter.

We are **CALM**, *yes?*.................**SMILE**................*breathe deeply and slowly.* We are still feeling the **PLEASURE** of reaching this level, and the **SATISFACTION** of being a better person, and our **WILLINGNESS** to reach our goal and to **ACHIEVE** a Good Life.

Look at the Map again..........see how far you have come since the level of trauma; it is only a memory, a thought form that needs to be **CLEARED** and to be **MERCIFUL** towards; you have **ELIMINATED, DESTROYED, ABDICATED, WITHDRAWN** and **RELEASED** it by moving so far away from it and into the higher emotions, that it no longer holds you in its power *(and it is real power, but not a high power)*.

Yet to turn and look back at the level that held those feelings, is to feel them again *(which is why we say, 'Don't look back at the bad stuff' .....until you have really Forgiven)*.

For your **FOCUS** upon anything, is the act of giving **ENERGY** to progress you..or defeat you...again!

To feel **CALM**, is to have shown **MERCY** to 'Yourself', not to anyone else! *(There is no Forgiveness you need to show them..................it is for YOU)!*

When you now look back, you feel **COMPASSION** towards anyone who hurt your feelings in the past, for they too are on a journey of discovery of Love and Happiness. Your judgement, blame and need for revenge about the experience, was more harmful to you than what they said or did.

Forgiveness **IS** to let the past go and move on to another higher level; and you may have found there is something to Forgive on every level, because you do not understand everything and so you make the mistakes to learn **Comparison** and **Choice**..again!

.

The Map of Ascension

Vibrational (Hz) levels of Emotion and how to get there...

Goal	Hz	Process
Unconditional Love	1000	100% Integrity
Peace	900	Compassion
Passion	800	Abundance
Bliss	750	Illumination
Joy	700	Trust
Love	650	Freedom
Learning	600	Gratitude
Happiness & Belief	**550**	**Worthiness**
Forgiveness & Positivity	500	Acceptance
Serenity	400	Pleasure
Hopefulness	300	Calm & Intention
boredom	***200***	Release
pride & scorn	175	inflation
hate & anger	150	aggression
craving & disappointment	125	enslavement
anxiety & fear	100	withdrawal
grief & regret	75	despondency
apathy & despair	50	helplessness
guilt & blame	30	destruction
shame & humiliation	20	elimination
sickness	10	Thankfulness
death	---	Want to Live

'Happiness and Belief' *given to you, by yourself, by your permission and perseverance in wanting the best for yourself.*

Once again...Look at the Map and see how far you have come........WOW!

That FEELS really good doesn't it.

This is the Process that takes you up into Happiness when you were feeling anxious or depressed, fearful or angry.

You are lucky enough to now, 'Know the Process'.
Some don't even know there is a Process!

Good thoughts create good ideas and solutions to life's problems, so it really is worth the effort to keep remaining in Happiness to make Life's right choices.

SMILE now...

SMILE again now...that takes you higher in feeling to the next level and your acceptance of good thoughts keeps you in the higher levels.

Throw away all lower feeling thoughts...any thought that feels bad keeps you in those lower emotions, and overcome them by choosing to think better of yourself and others for more good feeling thoughts.

It is always your choice to accept a Good or bad thought.

You have the choice, and so does everyone else!

WILLINGNESS favourably disposed or inclined; ready; cheerfully compliant; done; given; accepted; freely or voluntarily chosen...

the next level up...

.

The Map of Ascension

Vibrational (Hz) levels of Emotion and how to get there...

Goal	Hz	Process
Unconditional Love	1000	100% Integrity
Peace	900	Compassion
Passion	800	Abundance
Bliss	750	Illumination
Joy	700	Trust
Love	650	Freedom
Learning	**600**	**Gratitude**
Happiness & Belief	550	Worthiness
Forgiveness & Positivity	500	Acceptance
Serenity	400	Pleasure
Hopefulness	300	Calm & Intention
boredom	***200***	Release
pride & scorn	175	inflation
hate & anger	150	aggression
craving & disappointment	125	enslavement
anxiety & fear	100	withdrawal
grief & regret	75	despondency
apathy & despair	50	helplessness
guilt & blame	30	destruction
shame & humiliation	20	elimination
sickness	10	Thankfulness
death	---	Want to Live

'Learning' are you happy with all you know?
Do you think there is more for you to learn?
Why do you want to?

.

That's right, there are still more levels to get you higher than you are now, so there is still more to learn......*and how thankful are you for all you have already learnt so far?*

There is always more to learn.............in so many subjects that you enjoy. Keep to the subjects you enjoy for now, and if you still have time in your later life, you may then find room for subjects you thought you did not enjoy before, and you will find them more pleasurable; the learning actually keeps you alive, as you will find you still have more to do here.

ABSTRACTION is the process of formulating generalized concepts by extracting common qualities from specific examples =

"WHERE IS THE GOOD IN THIS MOMENT?"

"What can you be thankful for in this moment?"

Learning to Understand and Reason for Wisdom to be Meaningful.

GRATITUDE a feeling of thankfulness *FOR ALL THE GOOD THAT YOU HAVE NOW!*
to see the good in any situation you find yourself in, will **FEEL GOOD.**

Be thankful there is so much to learn, and in that feeling of *THANKS* you will enjoy learning so much more...it is the fastrack to Happiness

and rise up into the next level of...

.

The Map of Ascension

Vibrational (Hz) levels of Emotion and how to get there...

Goal	Hz	Process
Unconditional Love	1000	100% Integrity
Peace	900	Compassion
Passion	800	Abundance
Bliss	750	Illumination
Joy	700	Trust
Love	**650**	**Freedom**
Learning	600	Gratitude
Happiness & Belief	550	Worthiness
Forgiveness & Positivity	500	Acceptance
Serenity	400	Pleasure
Hopefulness	300	Calm & Intention
boredom	***200***	Release
pride & scorn	175	inflation
hate & anger	150	aggression
craving & disappointment	125	enslavement
anxiety & fear	100	withdrawal
grief & regret	75	despondency
apathy & despair	50	helplessness
guilt & blame	30	destruction
shame & humiliation	20	elimination
sickness	10	Thankfulness
death	---	Want to Live

'Love' .....*Oh, we have been waiting so long for you on this level, thanks for getting here now.*

LOVE, LOVE, LOVE...
The feeling of LOVE is one of the greatest feelings you will experience.

LOVE is the best of feelings.
LOVE is the feeling you give to others.
LOVE is the feeling you give to yourself.
LOVE is the feeling that creates a glorious life for you and removes all
lower emotions just by wanting to experience the emotion of LOVE.

There is no hurt and no pain when you are in LOVE.

So when you say you are broken hearted due to your lost LOVE,
then you are mistaken.
You have not lost LOVE...your belief in loss is what hurts you.
You have chosen a lower emotion than LOVE, and that is all you feel.
LOVE does not cause hurt.
Hurtful thoughts and judgement of your loved one, cause YOU hurt.

When you loved everything about them, you felt good in LOVE.
When you start to dislike an aspect about the one you LOVE, it is YOU
who falls out of LOVE with them and your loving thoughts have been
changed for a lower feeling thought that only causes YOU harm.

Your loved one will feel only confusion as to why you no longer show the
interest you once did, and so then they too start to judge you and your
behaviour
...and so you both fall out of LOVE with each other,
due to your changing your minds about each other.

And so, to fall back into LOVE with someone, is always a choice.

To feel good in LOVE is YOUR choice.

Do you want to think kind thoughts about a person ?
Do you want to say kind words about a person ?
Do you want to accept them as they are ?
Do you LOVE them the way they are ?

.

"Yes, but they said this, they did that...etc." You say...

And that has now past,
and we have already learnt Forgiveness haven't we!

It is always your choice to think a kind thought rather than accept a judgement thought about them.....

IS IT TRUE?
IS IT REALLY TRUE?

...REALLY?
and remember reality feels good!

You can only answer that by your past knowledge of kindness to others.

The Process to rise to the next level in **LOVE**,
is to give your partner their ***FREEDOM***,

FREEDOM *is personal liberty, as from slavery; liberation from bondage or confinement; the quality or state of being free; exemption or immunity; the right or privilege of unrestricted use or access; autonomy; independence; quality of the will of the individual of being unrestrained; ease of frankness of manner; ease and grace of movement.*

Allow them to be just as they always have been
...and if they choose to leave you,
just as you have the choice to leave them,
then LOVE them for being truthful,
and also wanting to LOVE themselves,
rather than hurt each other with judgements that you both have not learnt to control yet.

The Process to rise up from **Love** and into **Joy** is...

.

REVELATION *the act of disclosing something previously secret or obscured, especially something true; a fact revealed especially in a dramatic or surprising way.............................(just like finding this book!)*

And we have already learnt **Release**, **Forgiveness** and **Understanding**.

In Christianity, **Revelation** is God's disclosure of his own nature and his purpose for mankind.
To disclose divine truths, bring them to light and take pleasure in them.

Be thankful for the Goodness of the information,
and know that if the Goodness does not feel good,
it is only you who is judging the Goodness that is there in front of you.

So smile at your misunderstanding and be thankful for all the Good.

You are **Forgiven**, you just need to forgive yourself,
and that is easy when you **SMILE** and know that everything is Good,
NOW!

Shall we walk together, hand in hand, into Joy....
.
.
.
.
.
.
.
.

SMILE....*breathe slowly and deeply*..
.
.
.
.
.
.
.

The Map of Ascension

Vibrational (Hz) levels of Emotion and how to get there...

Goal	Hz	Process
Unconditional Love	1000	100% Integrity
Peace	900	Compassion
Passion	800	Abundance
Bliss	750	Illumination
Joy	**700**	**Trust**
Love	650	Freedom
Learning	600	Gratitude
Happiness & Belief	550	Worthiness
Forgiveness & Positivity	500	Acceptance
Serenity	400	Pleasure
Hopefulness	300	Calm & Intention
boredom	***200***	Release
pride & scorn	175	inflation
hate & anger	150	aggression
craving & disappointment	125	enslavement
anxiety & fear	100	withdrawal
grief & regret	75	despondency
apathy & despair	50	helplessness
guilt & blame	30	destruction
shame & humiliation	20	elimination
sickness	10	Thankfulness
death	---	Want to Live

'JOY' ...*are you still together in* **LOVE** *?*
or did you give them their Freedom ?

Did you give yourself your Freedom ?

Now you can really learn about JOY in a relationship...........let's see how...

.

JOY TO THE WORLD...

Your **Joy** can influence the whole World,
and when there are 2 of you in your **Joy**,
you are then bringing more **Joy** to the World.

And they then can influence their World too.
(just as we do when we are sad !).

Your relationship is not about the 2 of you becoming one person;
then you would only ever be half a person;
when you come to realize that you are still a single person in your
relationship, and you have **chosen** to stay together...

Now you understand how good **JOY** feels.

You are in **CONTROL** of your choices to **LOVE** and be **KIND** in
thought, word and deed, and that always feels fantastic;
as you have found another with the same ideals and beliefs as yourself and
you have more to give each other in Learning and **TRUST.**

TRUST *is reliance on and confidence in the truth, worth, reliability of a
person or thing; to have FAITH in; to expect, hope or suppose; the
obligation of someone in a responsible position; in charge, custody or care
of another; a person or thing in which confidence or faith is placed; an
arrangement whereby a person to whom the legal title to a property is
conveyed and holds such property for the benefit of those entitled to the
beneficial interest; to allow with confidence in good sense of honesty.*

When you fully **TRUST** another that feeling is **JOY**.

When you don't **TRUST** another you can still feel the **JOY**, because that
feeling can shift you into **TRUST**, and shifts their World to your level too.

...and when you feel **JOY** and **TRUST,** you are shifting upwards again
into **BLISS**.

.

If you have decided to journey alone to this emotional destination, then you perhaps have found it easier...Congratulations.

Sometimes it is easier to remain as a single childlike being, to feel the exhilaration, rather than remove all past programs of how to act as an adult.

And as with every level you have felt,
it is still Comparison.

You may then wish to 'go back' and find a partner with whom you can lead them into their **BLISS** too...

...and that is one of the greatest kindness's to give to another,
for them to experience the highest emotions with the **COMPASSION** and **TRUST** they also need to learn in this Life journey.

Thank you.

TRANSFIGURATION *a complete change of form or appearance into a more beautiful or spiritual state. To change your appearance to lift you up into **JOY** can be in any way that makes YOU feel good.*

And on to...

.

.

.

.

.

are you ready for it...?

.

.

.

.

The Map of Ascension

Vibrational (Hz) levels of Emotion and how to get there...

Goal	Hz	Process
Unconditional Love	1000	100% Integrity
Peace	900	Compassion
Passion	800	Abundance
Bliss	**750**	**Illumination**
Joy	700	Trust
Love	650	Freedom
Learning	600	Gratitude
Happiness & Belief	550	Worthiness
Forgiveness & Positivity	500	Acceptance
Serenity	400	Pleasure
Hopefulness	300	Calm & Intention
boredom	***200***	Release
pride & scorn	175	inflation
hate & anger	150	aggression
craving & disappointment	125	enslavement
anxiety & fear	100	withdrawal
grief & regret	75	despondency
apathy & despair	50	helplessness
guilt & blame	30	destruction
shame & humiliation	20	elimination
sickness	10	Thankfulness
death	---	Want to Live

'Bliss' ...*words cannot really explain the nature of Bliss...but you will know it when you are in it!*

ILLUMINATION the act of illuminating or the state of being illuminated; spiritual or intellectual enlightenment, insight or understanding; the act of making understood; clarification.

.

The Map of Ascension

Vibrational (Hz) levels of Emotion and how to get there...

Goal	Hz	Process
Unconditional Love	1000	100% Integrity
Peace	900	Compassion
Passion	**800**	**Abundance**
Bliss	750	Illumination
Joy	700	Trust
Love	650	Freedom
Learning	600	Gratitude
Happiness & Belief	550	Worthiness
Forgiveness & Positivity	500	Acceptance
Serenity	400	Pleasure
Hopefulness	300	Calm & Intention
boredom	***200***	Release
pride & scorn	175	inflation
hate & anger	150	aggression
craving & disappointment	125	enslavement
anxiety & fear	100	withdrawal
grief & regret	75	despondency
apathy & despair	50	helplessness
guilt & blame	30	destruction
shame & humiliation	20	elimination
sickness	10	Thankfulness
death	---	Want to Live

'PASSION' *is an ardent LOVE or affection; intense LOVE; a strong affection or enthusiasm for an object, concept etc.; any strongly felt emotion; the object of an intense desire; an outburst expressing intense emotion; easily aroused; quick tempered...***Passion***ate.*

The Illumination you experienced from the **BLISS**, will help you understand your **PASSION**, and your **WILLINGNESS** to want to return to help others, rather than remain up here, is hoped for and aided in ways you would never have imagined.

Your **PASSION** ...what is your true **PASSION** in life?
What have your learnt on your journey to this level of experience now ?
What makes you feel good just thinking about it ?
That internal smile and feel good factor that makes you want to rush back to the World and improve the lot of others.

That is **YOUR PASSION**.

Every time you think about it, you feel fantastic, and in that feeling you know you can complete the task you have accepted as **YOUR PASSION**. It was **your choice,** just as it is always your choice to feel good.

You had to feel good to realize your **PASSION** and your journey through life helped you to decide where your energy will be best used to help others...and yourself.

YOU are still the most important person to aid first, for without you and your feeling good, you will fail in your **PASSION**, for you are either in it...or not!
Just like with **LOVE**.
You choose to **LOVE**...
you choose to remain in your **PASSION** and to aid you to remain within your **PASSION** and to rise up to the next level you need to feel...

ABUNDANT *is a copious supply; a great amount; fullness or benevolence; a degree of plentifulness; affluence.*

And that can be in anything you feel you are **ABUNDANT** in....

Tea bags, shoes, paper, flowers, **LOVE**, Happiness, energy, anything...
Just to keep feeling Good in your multitude of *ABUNDANCE* will keep you in these higher levels of feeling good and stay in the levels of *SOLUTION* and success in your **PASSION**...............and then you are in...

.

The Map of Ascension

Vibrational (Hz) levels of Emotion and how to get there...

Goal	Hz	Process
Unconditional Love	1000	100% Integrity
Peace	**900**	**Compassion**
Passion	800	Abundance
Bliss	750	Illumination
Joy	700	Trust
Love	650	Freedom
Learning	600	Gratitude
Happiness & Belief	550	Worthiness
Forgiveness & Positivity	500	Acceptance
Serenity	400	Pleasure
Hopefulness	300	Calm & Intention
boredom	***200***	Release
pride & scorn	175	inflation
hate & anger	150	aggression
craving & disappointment	125	enslavement
anxiety & fear	100	withdrawal
grief & regret	75	despondency
apathy & despair	50	helplessness
guilt & blame	30	destruction
shame & humiliation	20	elimination
sickness	10	Thankfulness
death	---	Want to Live

'Peace' *has awakened within you, due to your wanting perfection in Self and others, as you understand we are all Well-Being and perfect, should we so choose.*

....and you FEEL really Peaceful thinking good thoughts and smiling.

.

Empathy and **Compassion** I have found and explained as this...

There is a hypothetical pit, with a person in it...

Empathy sees the person and gets into the pit,
to feel what it is like to be in the pit *(to learn and feel the Comparison),*
and then tries to get them both out of the pit.

Compassion has already learnt **Comparison** and already knows what it is like to be in the pit,
and how long it took to get out of the pit.
Compassion leans down and offers a hand to the person in the pit.
Whether the person takes Compassion's hand or not,
is the **choice** of the person in the pit.

The Compassionate live to help others...for longer!

You can go about your business, your life and your feelings remaining in Peace, when you understand that you have achieved a level where you actually choose to return to help others.

There are consequences of this returning to help others...
You lower your level to reach them.

The Art of Consciousness is to rise up again, to feel good helping others and hold on to your Happiness, knowing it is you who creates it.......on any level.

Use the tools... As in anything, there are tools.

Follow the Process...
and
* **SMILE** and **be thankful** for all the good in your life now.......**to rise up**.

* complain, judge, hate, worry, regret, anger, refuse etc..........to sink down.

Your feelings are your **Internal SatNav** and you are always, always using one of your emotional tools on your journey.........so feel good, and rise up.
.

The Map of Ascension

Vibrational (Hz) levels of Emotion and how to get there...

Goal	Hz	Process
Unconditional Love	**1000**	**100% Integrity**
Peace	900	Compassion
Passion	800	Abundance
Bliss	750	Illumination
Joy	700	Trust
Love	650	Freedom
Learning	600	Gratitude
Happiness & Belief	550	Worthiness
Forgiveness & Positivity	500	Acceptance
Serenity	400	Pleasure
Hopefulness	300	Calm & Intention
boredom	***200***	Release
pride & scorn	175	inflation
hate & anger	150	aggression
craving & disappointment	125	enslavement
anxiety & fear	100	withdrawal
grief & regret	75	despondency
apathy & despair	50	helplessness
guilt & blame	30	destruction
shame & humiliation	20	elimination
sickness	10	Thankfulness
death	---	Want to Live

'Unconditional Love' is...1000%

INTEGRITY *is adherence to moral principles; honesty; the quality of being unimpaired; soundness; unity; wholeness.*

.

Look at the word Unconditional...it is fantastic!

the **'U'** is a smile.

the **'n'** is a frown, an upside down smile.

Placed before the **'condition'**

...so its giving you the choice of thought,
and you then head in that direction.

* **SMILE** and rise Up

* complain, hate, judge, regret, despair, worry etc. to head downwards.

Both are necessary, as we cannot always be happy; as we then isolate ourselves from those who have as yet not found the Process, to their own Happiness.

.

.

.

AND WHY DO WE NEED TO KNOW THIS?

Feeling Good heals all the past damage that you have done to your body from the past...so you are in Good Health and renewing damaged cells quicker and with more Energy and Purity of Thought.

Perfection comes from perfected Thoughts,
and damaged thoughts create more damage.

There is no struggle in Good Thoughts, you **SMILE** and choose to think for the best, and so they are more forthcoming.
The **SMILE** is the tool to rise you up.

You will become more at ease with practice of the Process,
and you will only FEEL out of ALIGNMENT,
(with the goodness that you felt good in)
....as soon as you start to fall in thought again.
...so just **SMILE**.....................................There, that feels better.

EMOTIONAL SPIRAL

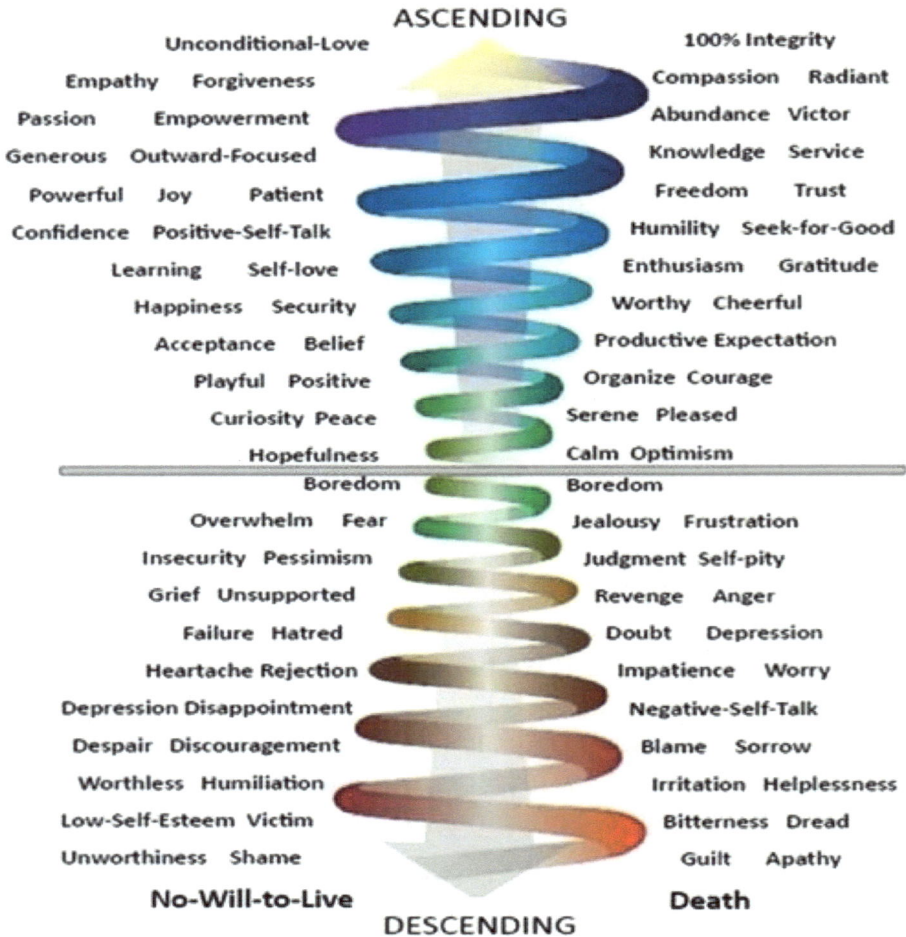

ASCENDING

Unconditional-Love	100% Integrity
Empathy Forgiveness	Compassion Radiant
Passion Empowerment	Abundance Victor
Generous Outward-Focused	Knowledge Service
Powerful Joy Patient	Freedom Trust
Confidence Positive-Self-Talk	Humility Seek-for-Good
Learning Self-love	Enthusiasm Gratitude
Happiness Security	Worthy Cheerful
Acceptance Belief	Productive Expectation
Playful Positive	Organize Courage
Curiosity Peace	Serene Pleased
Hopefulness	Calm Optimism
Boredom	Boredom
Overwhelm Fear	Jealousy Frustration
Insecurity Pessimism	Judgment Self-pity
Grief Unsupported	Revenge Anger
Failure Hatred	Doubt Depression
Heartache Rejection	Impatience Worry
Depression Disappointment	Negative-Self-Talk
Despair Discouragement	Blame Sorrow
Worthless Humiliation	Irritation Helplessness
Low-Self-Esteem Victim	Bitterness Dread
Unworthiness Shame	Guilt Apathy
No-Will-to-Live	**Death**

DESCENDING

WHY IT IS SO IMPORTANT TO UNDERSTAND JESUS CHRIST

Jesus was the man...

The Christ, is found in the positive, higher levels of this emotional scale
...Yay!

This is why He was different in that time of war and trouble,
and what He was trying to teach you...
about the frequency of LOVE and Peacefulness.

Higher levels of happiness create good days don't they!
When you are in alignment with your inner Christ, more good days
create a better life, friends, family and Good health.

...and demons/ the devil, are the negative lower thoughts and feelings in
the emotions...
they create more of the same in sickness and lack...
Oh dear, yes they do!

So to be in alignment with lower thoughts of judgement, complaint,
anger and fear...you create more of the same and hang around with
those kinds of people too.

Yes, the way things have been explained in the past, are so those who
could not read or understand emotional frequency and levels, would
think it was something OUTSIDE of themselves, so they could remain
fighting and believing in war

...rather than knowing that all they had to do was think a better feeling
thought, Smile, and accept that a life change will come when you
change your lower mind/emotions to a higher, better feeling thought,
a kindness, a good action, a peaceful word.

...and as the Law of Attraction states....'Like attracts Like'.

.
To remain in the lower levels, you become a lower emotional being with
all the sickness, anger, fear and lack that comes from that low
frequency.

So,
when you are happy, you attract other happy people,
just like Jesus did......Disciples of Happiness and Good attitude.

...or else the others crucify/harm you to get you out of their life
experience (rather than learn to change their beliefs and acceptance of
something different to themselves).

You can walk away,
and Jesus died to show an 'extreme example' of how these things work.

So,
it is a choice to be happy,
or live in fear...

There is nothing to fear,
...except those you experience fear with!

Life is a choice...
Smile, Feel Good and Believe in G(oo)dness... to go up!

complain, judge, hate, fear, condemn... to keep going down.
.
.
.
.
.
.
It is always your choice in everything you accept in thought.

Peace and Love be with you in your Smile.

Yogi Sally Ann Slight

QUESTION POSTED....Beautiful souls I would appreciate your wisdom please.

I'm on ACIM lesson 32, "I have invented the world I see"

I'm struggling with this. My son (11) is very poorly and very sad. I just can't seem to get my head around it... I haven't invented it; it's definitely there.

How can I see this differently please? And should I just carry on with the lessons although I seem to be stuck on this one?

Best wishes

.

.

.

REPLY......Paramahansa Yogananda taught us to surround the person with a thought of perfection; to see them surrounded by Love, Peace, Harmony, Joy and Calm.

By doing this you are actually focusing on what you want.... rather than what you perceive to be true at this time. To change your mind is to change your perception.

Love, Peace, Harmony, Joy and Calm never go away.... they are just on the other side of your attention, at the time of your lower thought.

So you turn to the Love, Peace, Harmony, Joy and Calm as soon as you feel/see anything that you do not feel good about......and only accept the good thought.

Turn away the lower thought by a good thought of Love, Peace, Harmony, Joy and Calm.

I have attached a Map so you can see where each of these emotions are...
and where you can also see the lower thought/emotions
that are not making you see correctly
the goodness that is always there.

When you are able to understand this correction,
you can then teach your son,
who will turn his thoughts around,
if he feels they are bothering him also.

Just as you have the right to change your mind....
so does he....
yet, if he does not know that he can (and how)
you may see more of the lower behaviour that not even your love can shift,
until he himself decides to change his own perception.

And that is what we are here to learn to do...
to learn and to teach what we have learnt;
for the good of the student,
rather than for the happiness of the Teacher.

Peace be with you and your family
16th July 2020

EMOTIONAL SPIRAL

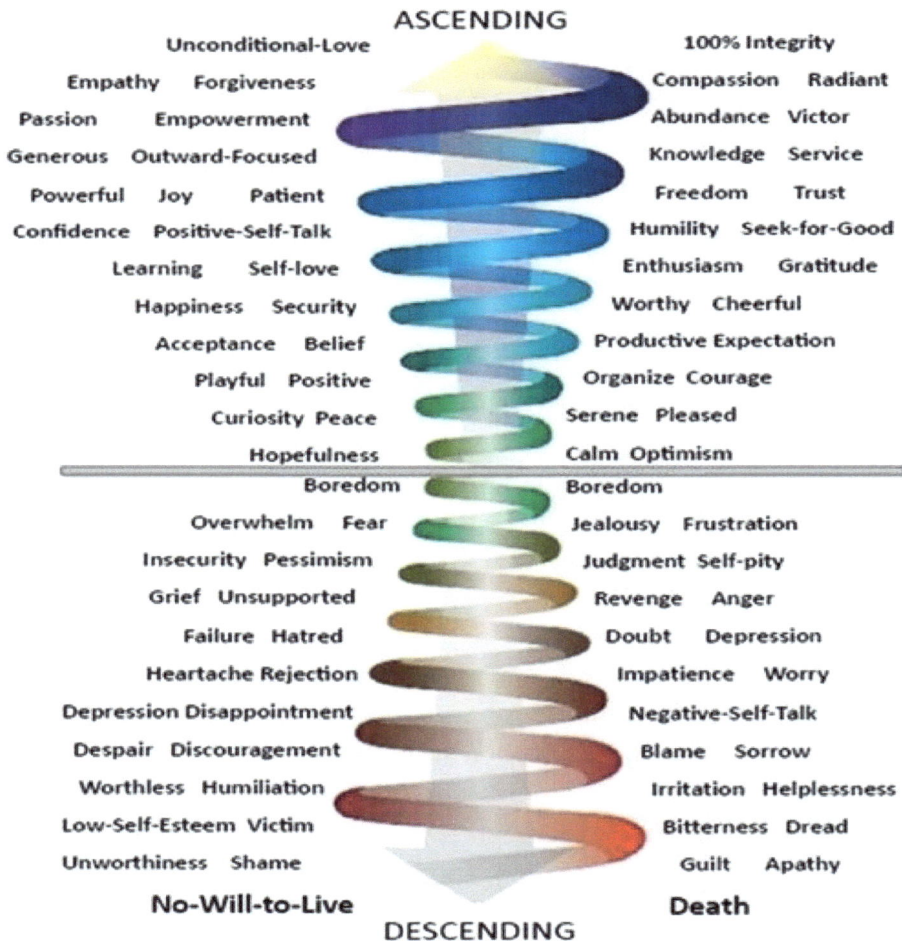

ASCENDING

Unconditional-Love

100% Integrity

Empathy   Forgiveness

Compassion   Radiant

Passion   Empowerment

Abundance   Victor

Generous   Outward-Focused

Knowledge   Service

Powerful   Joy   Patient

Freedom   Trust

Confidence   Positive-Self-Talk

Humility   Seek-for-Good

Learning   Self-love

Enthusiasm   Gratitude

Happiness   Security

Worthy   Cheerful

Acceptance   Belief

Productive Expectation

Playful   Positive

Organize Courage

Curiosity Peace

Serene   Pleased

Hopefulness

Calm Optimism

Boredom

Boredom

Overwhelm   Fear

Jealousy   Frustration

Insecurity   Pessimism

Judgment Self-pity

Grief   Unsupported

Revenge   Anger

Failure   Hatred

Doubt   Depression

Heartache Rejection

Impatience   Worry

Depression Disappointment

Negative-Self-Talk

Despair   Discouragement

Blame   Sorrow

Worthless   Humiliation

Irritation   Helplessness

Low-Self-Esteem   Victim

Bitterness   Dread

Unworthiness   Shame

Guilt   Apathy

No-Will-to-Live

Death

DESCENDING

Written by...

Yogi Sally Ann Slight
Dartmouth
Devon
UK

Yoga Life Coach & Good Health Motivator.
Yoga Siromani taught at Sivananda Ashram, Bahamas 2007.
Masseuse/Motivator to EDDIE KIDD (after his accident),
and the SUPER BIKERS at BRANDS HATCH Race Circuit, Kent,
Life Coach/Motivator to Servicemen with addictions & P.T.S.D.
and gives Solutions to questions on Facebook.

Just as Yoga Asana classes keep your body flexible and healthy, you also need a flexible mind to regain strength and happiness to improve your life situation.

To understand your emotions and feelings, and how to change them, will bring you great success in reaching any of your life ambitions or embarking upon a change in career...or enabling you to cope with loss or suffering from depression.

Health has a root, and the root is based within the mind, and when you are understanding your emotions you can then weed out sickness and negative paths and return your life of happiness.

You have the **CHOICE** to be happy or sad!
...it is a good habit that will give you the understanding to regain, and maintain, your health, happiness and success again.

Thank you for changing your Mind...Thank you!

www.ingramcontent.com/pod-product-compliance
Lightning Source LLC
Chambersburg PA
CBHW041524090426
42737CB00038B/111